news from nowhere,

present

a **news from nowhere** production

THE UNIVERSITY
WINCHESTER

ENGLAND

A PLAY FOR GALLERIES BY TIM CROUCH

Co-directors **Karl James** & **a smith**
Sound designer **Dan Jones**
Performers **Tim Crouch** & **Hannah Ringham**
Administrative producer **Lisa Wolfe**

Premiered at The Fruitmarket Gallery, Edinburgh, 4 August 2007

ENGLAND is a Traverse Theatre Company commission, co-produced by news from nowhere, Culturgest (Portugal) and Warwick Arts Centre. It is supported by Arts Council England, and the Peggy Ramsay Foundation and was partially developed at the National Theatre Studio.

Thanks

Philip Howard, Katherine Mendelsohn, Mike Griffiths and the staff of the Traverse Theatre. Fiona Bradley and the staff of The Fruitmarket Gallery. Purni Morell and the National Theatre Studio. Francisco Frazão and Margarida Mota at Culturgest. Alan Rivett and Neil Darlison at Warwick Arts Centre. Hannah Reade, Jane Prophet, Alex Hartley, Pooja Kumar, John Retallack, Peter Ursem, Helen Porter, Femi Elufowoju Jnr, Simon Fanshawe, the University of Sussex, Shunt, Shelley Hastings and BAC, Martin Platt and David Elliot at Perry Street Theatre in Exile, Greg Piggot, the Peggy Ramsay Foundation, Eleanor, Owen & Joe.

news from nowhere

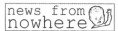

news from nowhere was established in 2003 to help produce
the work of Tim Crouch. Its ambition, sometimes, is to explore
the borders between theatre, visual art and education.

www.newsfromnowhere.net

Traverse Theatre

**The Traverse Theatre has established itself as Scotland's leading
exponent of new writing, with a reputation that extends worldwide.**
(*The Scotsman*)

From its conception in 1963, the Traverse's commissioning process embraces a spirit of
innovation and risk-taking that has launched the careers of many of Scotland's best-known
writers including John Byrne, David Greig, David Harrower and Liz Lochhead. It is unique in
Scotland as it fulfills the crucial role of providing the infrastructure, professional support and
expertise to ensure the development of a dynamic theatre culture for Scotland. Discover
more about the Traverse at www.traverse.co.uk

The Fruitmarket Gallery – showing world class art in the heart of the city.

The Fruitmarket Gallery brings artists and audiences together
through an internationally-renowned programme of exhibitions,
commissions, interpretation, education and publishing.

Exhibitions show new and existing work by Scottish and international artists in solo and group
presentations. Commissions enable artists to develop and make new work. Interpretation
gives audiences the tools to access art for themselves, encouraging questions and supporting
debate. Education explores issues raised in art with audiences of all ages, backgrounds and
knowledge levels. Publishing extends the reach of all of the Gallery's creative activity, in a
range of publications including free exhibition guides, inexpensive education publications,
exhibition catalogues, artist's books and limited edition artworks.

Culturgest

Culturgest is a cultural centre in Lisbon created in 1993 by the bank
Caixa Geral de Depósitos. It is devoted to the presentation of theatre,
dance, music and visual arts from both Portuguese and international artists, with a focus on
contemporary work.

In the last few years, Culturgest has presented or co-produced plays by Tim Crouch, Caryl
Churchill, Mark Ravenhill, Pier Paolo Pasolini, Luigi Pirandello, Miguel Castro Caldas and Will
Eno, along with work by companies such as Rimini Protokoll (Berlin), Elevator Repair Service
(New York) and Krétakör (Budapest).

www.culturgest.pt

Warwick Arts Centre

As the UK's largest arts venue outside London, Warwick Arts
Centre welcomes well over a quarter of a million visitors every
year to enjoy a diverse and exciting programme of performances,
music, exhibitions and films. It has an ongoing commitment to developing and showing the
very best contemporary theatre from both the UK and across the globe.

www.warwickartscentre.co.uk

Biographies

Tim Crouch (writer & performer)

Tim Crouch's first play, *My Arm*, opened at the Traverse Theatre in 2003 and has toured internationally with runs at the 59 East 59 Theatres in New York and BAC in London. His own adaptation for BBC radio won the 2005 Prix Italia for Best Adapted Drama. In 2005 he premiered *An Oak Tree* at the Traverse where it won a Herald Angel. *An Oak Tree* has toured extensively, with runs at the Soho Theatre, London, and the Barrow Street Theatre, New York, where it was awarded a Special Citation Obie.

Tim has also written successfully for young audiences. His play, *Shopping For Shoes*, commissioned by the National Theatre's Education Department, won the 2007 Brian Way Award for children's playwrighting. His trilogy of plays, *I, Shakespeare*, has run at the Unicorn Theatre in London and at both the Brighton Festival and the Bath Shakespeare Festival.

Tim was an actor and founder member of the Bristol theatre company, *Public Parts*. Acting credits include *Light Shining in Buckinghamshire*, *The Good Woman of Setzuan* and *Endgame* (with HMP Brixton) all for the National Theatre. Tim is an Associate Artist at the Franklin Stage Company, New York, where *My Arm* received its first reading and where his roles have included Malvolio in *Twelfth Night*, Petruchio in *The Taming of the Shrew*, Prospero in *The Tempest* and Vanya in *Uncle Vanya*.

www.newsfromnowhere.net

Hannah Ringham (performer)

Hannah Ringham studied fine art at Brighton University and performance at Central School of Speech and Drama. She is a co-founder of the Shunt Theatre Collective, with whom she has worked on every production: *The Ballad of Bobby Francois*, *Sightings*, *The Tennis Show*, *Dance Bear Dance*, *Tropicana* and *Amato Saltone* (the last two in collaboration with the National Theatre). Shunt's awards include the Peter Brook Empty Space 2005, the Time Out Live Award 2003 and a Herald Angel in 2000. Since 2006 the Shunt Vaults (under London Bridge station) have hosted the Shunt Lounge, where the company programmes different artists to try out new work.

Aside from Shunt, other collaborations include performing in *The Itch*, a film by Glen Neath, 2007, creating and performing *Ether Frolics* with Sound and Fury 2005 (Critics Choice), *Hedwig and Stoller*, a double act with David Rosenberg, a performer in *Oogly Boogly*, a show for 12–18 month olds created by Guy Dartnell and Tom Morris, singing in the band Superthriller who toured with Beck, and a guest actor in Tim Crouch's *An Oak Tree*.

www.shunt.co.uk

Karl James (co-director)

Karl's early working life was spent as an actor, composer and director working with (among others) John Retallack, Kenneth Branagh and Declan Donellan. With Tim Crouch, Karl produced and co-directed *My Arm* and co-directed *An Oak Tree*.

As director and founder of The Dialogue Project, most of Karl's time is spent helping people talk to each other. Recent projects include: *Braver Conversations*, a CD and audio installation commissioned by Unilever; *2+2=5*, a series of recorded conversations set to music; *Ideas That Can Change The World*, a collaboration with Creative Partnerships and The Helen Storey Foundation and a long term association with Educare Small School in Kingston.

In the last year, Karl has focused on the subject of Pain and in October 2006 brought together a priest, a dominatrix, a self-harmer, a bereavement counsellor and a burns victim to cross-fertilise their experiences and thoughts at a Round Table in France, the results of which formed a piece called *Intimate Conversations* for the Latitude Festival (2007).

www.thedialogueproject.com

a smith (co-director)

a smith is a UK-born artist based in Oslo. He has made work for the theatre, the gallery, the street, the page, the internet, and the classroom.

In 2006 he made *The Ibsen Hut*, a public project which travelled throughout Norway and recieved its final performances at The National Theatre, Oslo as part of Ibsen festival 2006. His current work includes *hvor er du? (where are you?)*, an interactive work for young people, and *innvandrer (immigrant)*, a solo performance which will premiere in October 2007.

He was a co-director on Tim Crouch's *An Oak Tree*. Other recent collaborations as a director include work with the Norwegian contemporary music ensemble NING, and a new solo performance by Rasmus Jørgensen.

www.asmithontheinternet.com

Dan Jones (sound designer)

Dan Jones is a British composer and sound designer working in film and theatre.

His film scores include *Shadow of the Vampire* (starring John Malkovich and Willem Dafoe) and Menno Meyjes' *Max* (starring John Cusack), for which he received the Ivor Novello Award for Best Film Score, 2004. He has written for all the major British television broadcasters and his TV work includes Sir David Attenborough's *The Life of Mammals*, the BBC series *Strange*, Pawel Pawlikowski's drama *Twockers* and Francesca Joseph's *Tomorrow La Scala*. He collaborated with Sebastião Salgado, John Berger and Paul Carlin on the BBC Arena special *The Spectre of Hope*.

Dan has also created music and soundscapes for large scale public artworks. He is the co-creator of Sky Orchestra where music is played from seven hot air balloons positioned over a city, making it one of the largest sound works in the world. His music has also been used by the Rambert Dance Company, The European Space Agency and was incorporated in Isaac Julien's *Paradise Omeros* which is exhibited at Tate Modern, London.

He is a founder member and co-artistic director of Sound and Fury Theatre Company whose productions pioneer the immersive use of experimental sound design.

Lisa Wolfe (administrative producer)

Lisa Wolfe is an independent arts producer, manager and administrator. As well as news from nowhere, she also works with comedy theatre company Spymonkey, dance/film-artists Liz Aggiss and Billy Cowie, and for the disability arts organisation Carousel. Lisa was previously Performing Arts and Drama Officer at Arts Council England, South East and spent a decade heading the marketing department for Brighton Festival.

This text was correct at the time of going to print but may differ from the text as performed.

Tim Crouch

ENGLAND

OBERON BOOKS
LONDON

First published in 2007 by Oberon Books Ltd
521 Caledonian Road, London N7 9RH
Tel: 020 7607 3637 / Fax: 020 7607 3629
e-mail: info@oberonbooks.com
www.oberonbooks.com

A catalogue record for this book is available from the British
Library.

ISBN: 1 84002 799 1 / 978 1 84002 799 0

Cover photograph by Steve Payne of *The Heart* by Jane Prophet,
silver on copper-plated Rapid Prototype of healthy human heart.

Cover design by julia@we3.co.uk

Printed in Great Britain by Antony Rowe Ltd, Chippenham

to Julia

'One has to have died already to be there.'

Brian O'Doherty
Inside the White Cube

A slash '/' indicates overlapping dialogue – the point when the next speaker begins their line.

Act One

Dabbing

A room in an art gallery (in this case, the Fruitmarket Gallery in Edinburgh) containing an exhibition of artwork (in this case, by Alex Hartley).

Two actors as guides – one male and one female.

Until the guides begin to speak, the only focus for the audience is the exhibition of artwork.

Thank you.

Thanks very much.

Thanks.

Ladies and gentlemen.

Thank you.

If it weren't for you, I wouldn't be here.

You saved my life!

Welcome to the Fruitmarket Gallery here in Edinburgh.

World class contemporary art at the heart of the city.

(We'll be here for around twenty-five minutes and then we'll go to another room.

Where we can sit down.)

As the name suggests, the building we are in was built as a fruit and vegetable market in 1938.

The Scottish Arts Council converted the market into a visual arts space in 1974.

This is the space we're in now.

Look.

It's beautiful.

Thank you Scottish Arts Council. If it weren't for you, we wouldn't be here.

You saved our lives!!

The Fruitmarket doesn't only exhibit work by Scottish artists, but also work by artists from all around the world – Chinese, Danish, German, Australian, Japanese, Italian, French, Russian, Canadian, Israeli, Icelandic, Dutch, Portuguese.

And, of course, American.

This current exhibition is of work by an artist called Alex Hartley.

Alex is English.

I hope you will make time while you're in Edinburgh to get to know Alex's work.

Please don't touch anything.

I'm also English.

My boyfriend is American.

But he's actually Dutch.

No one in America is really American!

My boyfriend has three passports.

He calls me kiddo.

'Hey kiddo!'

Hoe doet u, kiddo?

Ik ben zeer goed, dank u!

My boyfriend can speak four different languages. He's a citizen of the world!

I have no languages.

Everyone speaks English!

A sound starts. There is an underscoring from now to the end of act one – drifting in and out, building towards the end.

We live in London.

We love London!

We love London!

It's such a great place to live.

The city is dynamic and progressive. But it's so expensive. I couldn't afford to live here if it wasn't for my boyfriend.

My boyfriend buys and sells art for other people. He tells them what to buy – what's up and what's down. He travels the world. He's never been to the Fruitmarket Gallery. He'd love it if he came here.

He'd think it was fantastic. He'd love all these clean lines.

My boyfriend and I have been together for eight years.

Which is pretty fantastic, too!

He saved my life.

If it weren't for him, I wouldn't be here.

Look!

Look!

Here you can see me in the night.

Here you can see me leaning.

Here you can see me in the early morning.

Look. I've been sleeping on the sofa.

Look.

Look!

This is the view out there.

Look at the sun from the windows.

Look how the reflections from the buildings around us convey a sense of depth.

Look! My skin is damp with sweat.

Look!

I've left a stain on the fabric of the sofa!

My boyfriend's about to go to an art fair in Munich. He says it's like a yard sale. He's looking for Gothic woodcuts.

He has a client in Pennsylvania who is building a Bavarian Schloss.

A castle outside Pittsburgh!

Look.

Look!

Here he is giving me a glass of water.

Here he is saying to me that I should have woken him.

'Take a day off!' he's saying.

His skin is smooth.

He's going to Munich!

Munich is a thousand miles away.

I'm curled up on the sofa.

Look.

I'm so small.

Something's wrong.

Something's wrong with me.

The tone of the sound changes.

This is where we live, my boyfriend and me.

We live in Southwark. / Here.

/ We live in a converted jam factory / in Southwark.

/ Here, in Southwark. In / London.

/ In England.

We have a duplex.

We have white walls.

It's like heaven here!

Here.

Here.

We don't have much here, but what we have is pretty amazing.

We have a Marcus Taylor on the wall. He's a favourite of ours. His colours are amazing.

My boyfriend believes that art shouldn't just be in galleries. / It belongs in people's everyday lives.

/ Art is for all!

He's not a collector. He just gets what he likes.

We have a Gregory Crewdson and a small Gary Hume.

We have a Marc Quinn and a Tacita Dean.

In the other room, seriously, we have a small Willem de Kooning. / Seriously.

/ Seriously. It's not a joke.

Nobody believes us when we say it's the real thing.

They think it's a fake, but it's not!

We have a certificate.

Some people think that I did it!

Do I look like an artist?

We regulate the temperature and humidity.

Look.

De Kooning is one of the most famous American painters in the world.

One of the most famous painters in the world!

He is an abstract expressionist.

He was born in Rotterdam in 1904 but he came to America when he was twenty-two.

He was an immigrant.

He died in 1997. He had Alzheimer's. Some people say he got it from all the lead in the paint he used.

Art is deadly!

My boyfriend bought the painting at auction in 1995
– from a Swiss collector.

With a little bit of help from his father.

It's always good to buy art just before the artist dies, because after they die it goes up in value.

When they're dead, we know for sure they won't be able to paint any more!

Thank God!

The painting is unfinished, from a series of two studies for a canvas he did in 1952. My boyfriend paid an arm and a leg for it, but he loves de Kooning. My boyfriend's father is from Rotterdam, too, so that's why. Friends say we should put it in safe storage. But it's insured for a million pounds, which is more than twice what he paid for it at auction in 1995 from a Swiss collector.

It's worth more than this duplex!

And it's not even finished!!

Can you imagine?

I get scared to touch it.

Don't touch it, kid!

Raak het niet, kid!

Het is heel wat geld waard!

My boyfriend understands the market.

My boyfriend says that he can still smell the jam.

In the corners!

If you look at the lintel above the door, you can see the imprint of the architect – the set-square, the compass and the pyramid.

There used to be a wall here.

We don't make jam!

I've had a bad / night again.

/ This is leasehold.

Silence.

There are postcards / in the bookshop.

/ I can't concentrate.

The sound resumes.

My boyfriend's back from Munich now. He was outbid for a Dürer by a dealer from Osaka.

He's angry that he missed it.

He's grumpy with me.

Fucking Japs, he says!

He hates / it when I'm ill.

/ He wants us to make love, but I don't feel well enough.

My skin / is sore.

/ Not now.

I'm never ill!

Look.

I'm sorry.

He's pretending that it doesn't matter, but I know that it does.

Look.

Where's my / strength gone?

/ Where's my?

Where?

Can't lift / my feet.

/ Can't get to the bathroom in the night.

Please don't get the wrong idea about my boyfriend, though. I'm embarrassed that you should see him like this. / He's a really good guy.

/ He believes in art!

We have a Marc Quinn!

I feel inadequate next to him.

Look.

I'm useless. What's happening to me? Something's wrong with me! I'm worried that he will become distant towards me.

Look.

I love him so much. I lie awake and listen to my boyfriend breathing. I listen to the horses galloping in my chest. I feel all alone in the world. I wonder what it would be like to be dead. I hate it when my boyfriend doesn't get what he wants. I wonder if everything stops. I wonder if there's an afterlife. There must be. All this beauty can't just stop, can it!

All these clean lines!

Here.

Here in the Fruitmarket Gallery.

My boyfriend's father is Presbyterian. His company donates ten per cent of its profits to the church.

He sponsored a sculpture park for a cancer ward in Atlanta in Georgia.

My boyfriend's father did well in America.

He puts back what he gets out!

He won't come here, / though.

/ Look at the photographs.

Look at the floor! When we bought this place it was photographs of wood made to look like real wood! We replaced it with real wood!

Look.

My boyfriend has been to Korea.

He's been / to Lahore.

/ To Beijing.

To Madrid.

To Venice.

He's buying and selling!

Art is universal.

Here you can see my boyfriend talking on the phone. He's talking to a colleague in Zurich. I don't understand a word he's saying.

He's my lover and I don't understand what he's saying to his colleague in Zurich!

I don't have any languages.

His eyes are red from travelling. I don't think it's too late here. Maybe about 9. Or 9:30 maybe. Or later. Or earlier. Look at the light on the bookshelf. He brought it back from Japan.

Look at the angles / and the parallel lines.

/ Look at the light.

Look.

My boyfriend is so strong. When he holds me I feel his strength come into me.

My boyfriend is wearing a new belt.

He's travelling.

Air travel is so cheap!

My boyfriend laughs with his hands inside his pockets.

If you look, I'm going to the doctors. It's a beautiful day in Southwark in London. From where we're standing, we can see the Tower of London, Tower Bridge, the new County Hall, the Gherkin.

Note also Guys Hospital, the Battleship HMS Belfast, the Globe Theatre and the tower of Tate Modern. So much to see it turns my head.

I used to like it when everything moved so quickly, but now I get dizzy.

My ankles are swollen. / Look.

/ I'm tired.

This isn't / my skin!

/ This isn't me.

This isn't me.

Our apartment is really near here! Near the water. Southwark has really seen a regeneration in recent years. / Property is so expensive.

/ It can't stay like that forever.

In 2006, a whale was spotted as far upstream as Chelsea!

A whale in central London! As my boyfriend would say, Wie dat zou geloven?!

Wie dat zou geloven?!

This is my doctor's surgery. / It's near London Bridge.

/ It's bright and airy.

On the walls are prints by Raoul Dufy, David Hockney and Seurat.

A translation service is available.

Look.

Look.

The patients like to look at the paintings. It helps them to feel better about their illnesses.

Near my doctor's surgery is a place called Vinopolis
– which has wine from all over the world. People can go on guided tours through the wine cellars under a viaduct built in 1866. My boyfriend and I did that. We love wine. We love Vinopolis. Vinopolis started in 1999. 1999 is when me and my boyfriend got together.

On New Year's Eve!

The New Millenium.

Happy New Year!

Sit up here.

Breathe in.

Listen.

Breathe in.

Listen.

Listen again.

Look.

I'm a good patient.

This is cashmere!

Dr Kumar is sympathetic.

He asks me about my family.

He asks me about / my next of kin.

/ My boyfriend is my next of kin.

This is Southwark Cathedral. I like to come here when I've been to the doctor's. Here or to the Tate Modern gallery, which is only about just a stone's throw from here. From / Southwark Cathedral.

/ Here.

Doctor Kumar is my GP. He's great. If it weren't for him I wouldn't be here. But sometimes I can't understand what he's saying. It's frustrating. Especially if you are a doctor and need to say things clearly about how people are and how / people are feeling.

/ There's no room for ambiguity in the medical profession!

It's not an art form!

I have a stabbing pain!

I have a shooting pain!

I have a burning pain!

I think Southwark Cathedral is my favourite cathedral.

I used to bring my boyfriend here.

It's a good place for me to sit and think about things.

Here in Southwark Cathedral.

I enjoy the peace. I enjoy the clean lines and the feel and look of the stone.

Everyone talks so quietly.

It's beautiful.

It's like heaven.

Look.

We're standing now in the Nave.

Notice the central boss, in the form of a shield supported by angels. On this shield you can see the symbols of our Lord's suffering, / the nails, the crown of thorns, the scourge and the cross.

/ I feel like I'm sliding around. / I feel swollen up. I feel beached.

/ These are the works of an artist on the wall and in the cathedral.

This is art.

Look at me!

Look.

Here comes my boyfriend again. He's on the way to Istanbul, with a shopping list. He knows so much. He's learning Chinese.

I am in such pain here! It comes over me. Look.

Look at the colours in the corners of the eyes!

Look at my / fingernails!

The half moons!

My boyfriend sits by me. He feels for me so much that he doesn't want to leave me. But someone's got to support how we live. Look.

I'm bringing out my boyfriend's religious side. He used to be agnostic.

He never used to pray. And now he prays for me!

I must be in trouble!

All this is art.

All this is art.

This is how we look.

Look.

We're a couple.

When I'm with my boyfriend I think that anything is possible.

I feel indestructible!

I wish that I wasn't so ill so that we could have sex.

We used to have / really good sex.

/ I don't feel erotic.

He knows so much about art, which is why he would love
it here, in the Fruitmarket Gallery in Edinburgh. I don't
know anything, really. I look at these things and I don't
really understand them. I like them, but my boyfriend
would understand them. He would interpret them for me.

He says that good art is art that sells.

He's taught me the difference between looking and seeing!

This is Guys Hospital in London.

Look.

Look.

Look at the atrium.

Look at the clean lines.

I'm on the art trail. It connects the works of art in the
hospital, with information about the artists and the
therapeutic benefits of art in health.

This work is called 'African Woman With Child'.

It's beautiful.

Don't / touch it!

/ Even clean hands leave marks and damage surfaces!

My boyfriend would love it here in Guys Hospital. He would love the quiet and the spirit of the hospital. He would recognise the importance of art in recuperation and contemplation.

Art can make you feel better about going to die.

It can make you live longer!

Can you imagine?

Thanks, art!

If it weren't for you we wouldn't be here.

You saved our lives!

Doctor Frempong is a great man. He's always optimistic! / Look what he did for me!

/ He took a photograph of / my heart!

/ My arteries!

He saved my life. If it weren't for him, I wouldn't be here. Doctor Frempong comes from Ghana. His family still lives there.

Doctor Frempong tells me to smile with my heart!

I need this rail to keep my balance!

Guys Hospital was founded in 1719.

17 / 24.

/ 1721.

Guys Hospital was / founded.

/ This is in August.

This is August.

Atrial Fibrillation is when the atria and the ventricles of the heart beat at a different rate. This causes an abnormal rhythm of the heart, an arrhythmia, leading to palpitations, weakness, shortness of breath and dizziness.

I've been on the sofa again.

These bricks are original!

If you look closely you can see the chest heave and gallop.

I'm by the window.

There's no whale in the river today!

My boyfriend is going to Moscow.

This is the / bathroom.

/ I've been throwing up!

I'm in a car!

Look at the juxtaposition!

We're making plans.

Look / at the tones.

/ Any questions?

Gifts and books are in / the gift shop.

/ The café is closed.

Because of this.

My boyfriend and I are discussing arrangements.

Look.

I will want to be buried.

I will decide on which music to / be played.

/ Which poem is to be read.

I will want to be burnt.

My boyfriend doesn't want to talk about it. He doesn't
believe it will happen.

He's death-defying!

I'm so tired.

I can't breathe.

Look how small / I have become!

/ I'm disappearing!

Look at the shallowness of my breathing.

Look at the pulse at the side of my head.

Look at the weakness.

Listen to the helicopter blades.

Everything is an effort.

Look!

My skin is grey!

My boyfriend is amazing. He makes me feel safe.

Alex Hartley is a leading artist. As well as the Fruitmarket
here in Edinburgh and the Victoria Miro gallery in
London, he has exhibited at the Louisiana Museum of
Modern Art in Denmark, the Museum of Contemporary
Art in Sarajevo, the Distrito Cuatro in Madrid, the

Kunstlerhaus in Dortmund and the National Museum of Art in Osaka, Japan.

In 2004 Alex claimed sovereignty of a new Arctic island in the region of Svalbard in Norway. Revealed by the melting of the Arctic ice, the chunk of rock measures the size of a football pitch.

Alex has given it the name Nymark, which means 'new world' in Norwegian.

As the ice melts, he says, new landscapes emerge.

The symptoms of Hypertrophic Cardiomyopathy can develop very suddenly. Every possible avenue of treatment is explored before the issue of transplant is addressed.

Here I am at a hospital near Cambridge. My boyfriend drove me here.

This is in the countryside.

My boyfriend is shouting.

We are in a car park.

I am shaking.

Look.

The colours are bright.

It's a beautiful day.

Look.

The leaves are leaving the branches.

Everything is spinning away from me.

It's beautiful.

This is in London or in Southwark.

My boyfriend is on the phone to his father. His father runs a company in Atlanta. My boyfriend's father's company in Atlanta makes components in Atlanta Georgia.

My boyfriend's father is talking to his son about what is to be done. / They talk in English and in Dutch.

/ I don't understand them.

When my boyfriend is on the phone to his father he looks so cute. / He calls him 'sir'. Americans are so respectful.

/ My boyfriend says that this shouldn't be happening to us! That we should have gone private. That we're going to fight this. Here he is telling me that he loves me.

Look.

Look.

This is waiting.

Silence.

We're waiting.

Sound resumes.

My cardiologist is called Mrs Raad. She is from the Lebanon. If it weren't for her, / I wouldn't be here.

/ She saved my life.

Mrs Raad reminds us that the waiting list is horizontal.

She reminds us to pack a bag.

She reminds us to be ready.

She reminds us to keep the pager on for when a new heart is coming.

We're waiting.

Artwork can bring many therapeutic benefits to patients, visitors and staff within a hospital environment.

My boyfriend's father runs a company in Atlanta.

My boyfriend's father recommends a friend of a friend who might be able to help. He says that America has a lot of friends. / He is just like his son.

/ He's so positive.

My boyfriend is standing on our balcony with the phone. The phone is tucked under his chin. He is watching the river / and talking to a man 4000 miles away.

/ I am in bed with my / oxygen.

/ My boyfriend and my boyfriend's father pray for me down the telephone lines, through the microwaves.

Look.

I can't concentrate.

Look!

My skin is shedding.

/ I'm dying.

/ I'm dying.

I am led to understand by the people we have talked / to that this is it.

/ I understand this.

This is.

Everything is packing up! Look.

Look!

It's / so beautiful.

/ It's so frightening.

At night.

Here you can see me in the early morning.

Whatever.

Whatever.

Is.

Is this.

This.

Something.

Happening.

Look at the muscles in the heart. Look at them thickening. Look at how the pumping chamber gets smaller and keeps the heart muscle from relaxing properly between contractions. Look how the chambers of the heart stiffen as the muscle thickens.

It's happening to me here.

This is the picture.

Look!

Look!

I'm ready.

I'm ready even.

Ready.

What's / one less?

/ Really.

What's one less?

I will die either from sudden collapse, collapse without warning due to a collapse from sudden and severe arrhythmia. Or my heart will just fail in its job of pumping oxygenated blood around my body and I will pass into an unconsciousness and I will die.

I hope it will be sudden. Out in a blaze of glory.

Come on.

This way / please.

/ Follow me.

This is us waiting.

My boyfriend has spilt his wine.

My boyfriend is crying.

My boyfriend is / angry.

/ Is standing.

Is tensing.

Is.

My boyfriend is.

Look at the angles.

He says I have become defeatist.

That is defeatist talk.

I am being strong for him.

This is in Edinburgh.

It's maybe 8:20. Or 8:30.

Look at the light from the window.

The gallery will be closing.

I don't believe the phone will ring.

My beeper will not beep.

I don't know what will happen. Just nothingness, I suppose.
There was me and / then there was not me.

/ There was me and then there was not me.

In Munich.

In Madrid.

In Osaka.

In Oslo.

In Rotterdam.

In Berlin.

In Kabul.

In Edinburgh.

It's good that my boyfriend can't hear me talking like this.

He believes that anything is possible.

He believes in art.

If I died, I think my boyfriend would move back to the States.

People don't stay in foreign countries forever. At some point they get a call deep inside them to go back to their homeland. The place they understand.

Their heartland.

My heartland is here.

We are all at the / end of our

/ At the end of / our

/ End of

Our / patience.

/ My boyfriend has lost his / patience, too.

/ At the end of our patience with / everything.

/ He's losing everything.

It is not civilised.

To be like this.

To sit like this.

To grip like this.

To shake like this.

I was not led to believe that it would / be like this.

/ My boyfriend likes to be in control, but / he can't be.

/ This is intolerable.

He's having an outburst.

He says this wouldn't happen in the United States of America.

I'm / sorry.

/ I'm so sorry.

You shouldn't / have to see this.

/ I've really failed, haven't I? I've failed.

I'm so / so sorry.

/ I really really fucked up everything.

Everything.

I do not want / to be here.

/ This is not the right place to be.

Nowhere is the / right place to be.

/ There is no place to accommodate how I am and how I feel.

I don't like you to see my boyfriend like this. He's such a great guy. He's just at the end of his tether, to see his loved one like this.

He said he'd do / anything for me.

He'd do anything for me.

Anything.

Any.

Any.

Any questions?

I think I DO want to die.

The sound nearly reaches a climax.

The sound stops abruptly.

The sound of rooks and birdsong.

We're standing in the grounds of a stately home in the Royal County of Berkshire.

Look.

It's beautiful. A real English autumn afternoon.

Look.

I'm not too good in this cold air.

I'm not standing. I'm in a wheelchair! My boyfriend is behind me!

My oxygen is in a cradle at the back of my chair.

This building was designed in 1768 for the Earl of Renfrewshire. It's beautiful.

The house that you see today is a result of changes made in 1830 when the west wing was gutted by fire. In the rebuild, the architect transformed the main façade in the Indian style – adding the domes and minarets that give the house its distinctive appearance today.

The building has been a private residence, a hotel and a conference centre. In 2004 it was purchased by an international consortium.

Architecture is like a living organism, adapting to the culture of its time. Nobody wants to live in a museum.

We're here to see a leading heart surgeon who has agreed to see what he can do for me. It helps to have a rich boyfriend.

On the walls of the clinic are a genuine Bridget Riley, a Damien Hirst spin painting and a photograph by Sam Taylor-Wood. Don't touch them.

It's so beautiful.

It's so beautiful.

It's like being in a church. Or in a gallery. Everyone talks so quietly. Everything is so clean.

The end of the world.

Act Two

Wringing

A different room in the gallery.

Seats for the audience.

The wife is us, the audience. When the audience enter the space, it is her entering the space. The Interpreter interprets her words and translates what is said to her.

ENGLISH   Thank you.

INTERPRETER   Thank you.

ENGLISH   Thank you!

              If it weren't for you I wouldn't be here!

INTERPRETER   If it weren't for you I wouldn't be here.

ENGLISH   You saved my life!!

INTERPRETER   You saved my life.

ENGLISH   Look!

INTERPRETER   Look.

Silence.

ENGLISH   Never thought I'd be here. Never thought I'd see this or meet you or anything, really! It's amazing!! People at home think I'm crazy but I've been imagining this. Since I was ill. You know? Imagining coming here. Meeting you. Thanking you face-to-face.

> I am so grateful to you. And honoured to meet you.
>
> It is an honour to meet you!

INTERPRETER   I never thought I'd meet you.

ENGLISH   I've brought something for you. A gift to say thank you. Thank you to you!

> From me. For me! For my life!

INTERPRETER   It's an honour to meet you. I have a gift to thank you.

Silence.

ENGLISH   Would she like some refreshments ask her? Would she like some tea? Or a Coke?

> There's a machine out in the corridor. Or we could phone room service.
>
> I could easily and there's ice. There's ice in the corridor.

> Are they allowed Coke?

Silence.

> I can't thank her enough, tell her.

INTERPRETER   Would you like something to drink?

> I didn't want to see you. I didn't want anything to do with you. When I thought about you I felt sick. But then I spoke to my brother and he told me it would be the best thing. It would help me to move, to move forward.

> I didn't think I could look at you.

My brother lives in Australia. In Sydney. I haven't seen my brother.

This hasn't been an easy time for me. My family aren't together.

My cousin won't see you. He'll wait in the lobby until we've finished and then he'll take me back. I can't travel on my own.

Why has this happened to my family?

Why has this happened?

I want to know why this has happened to me.

I want to know if you have an answer.

ENGLISH   I understand.

INTERPRETER   I understand.

ENGLISH   I am so sorry for your loss.

INTERPRETER   I'm sorry for your loss.

ENGLISH   It must have been unbearable.

I was ill. In my country, tell her.

INTERPRETER   I was ill.

ENGLISH   Very ill. I was going to die. You wouldn't recognise me! The doctors couldn't help me. I was like this!

Tell her.

INTERPRETER   I was going to die.

ENGLISH   Look, I am well again. Look. It's a miracle!

INTERPRETER   I am well now.

ENGLISH   I take a lot of pills! But look! So far so good. The doctors say I'm doing very well, tell her! Look!

I'm jogging now. Run a marathon!

INTERPRETER   I am well now.

ENGLISH   I understand if it is difficult for her.

It was difficult to find you! To find you!

Does she understand anything?

Yes. Find you.

INTERPRETER   You were difficult to find.

ENGLISH   I hope this place is alright for her – It was / recommended by the Embassy –

INTERPRETER   / It's fine.

ENGLISH   I didn't know where we should meet, you know, somewhere neutral.

INTERPRETER   It's not an issue. / This is fine.

ENGLISH   / It's clean at any rate. Same all over the world!

Horrible lighting!

Silence.

Your husband – Hassam.

INTERPRETER   Your husband, Hassam.

ENGLISH   Hassam. Does she understand anything?
Your husband. Hassam. What was he like?

INTERPRETER   What was your husband like?

ENGLISH   What did he like? What did he do?

INTERPRETER   He was a good man. He loved me. He
loved his country. He loved this world. He
was twenty-six. He was just a good man.

ENGLISH   Of course. I'm sorry.

Is she – ?

I wanted to ask a question about her
husband.

Tell her.

INTERPRETER   I want to ask a question about Hassam.

ENGLISH   I wanted to ask – Did he – ? This is stupid,
tell her.

INTERPRETER   Carry on.

ENGLISH   Since the operation, I've been having weird
dreams – with snakes and elephants and
monkeys, you know. I thought maybe,
because of the – Did your husband, ask
her, did Hassam – did he work with
animals? Only I thought – You know you
hear of people -

INTERPRETER   Did Hassam work with animals?

He was going to college. He wanted to
study to be an engineer. He wanted to
go to university. He was a computer

programmer. He had sponsorship to go to college. To be an engineer.

ENGLISH Good. Good. Great!

We were – I was told very little. It's very good to meet her you.

I'm so sorry.

I have a tissue if –

Look. If this isn't convenient –

INTERPRETER Are you okay?

ENGLISH Yes, 'okay'?

INTERPRETER One moment please.

ENGLISH Of course.

INTERPRETER Of course.

Silence.

ENGLISH We could go outside?

INTERPRETER It's fine.

ENGLISH Must be weird for her, seeing me.

Silence.

It's cold. You don't really associate this part of the world with cold.

INTERPRETER This is winter.

ENGLISH Of course.

Silence.

This isn't what I expected, though. This traffic.

Could be anywhere.

My car's at 4.

Where are you from?

INTERPRETER Manchester.

ENGLISH Right.

Cold in Manchester!

When do you go back?

INTERPRETER I live here.

ENGLISH Here! Bloody hell! Good on you!

Can we turn this up?

INTERPRETER I can call the desk.

ENGLISH Don't bother.

What a place.

I don't think I could live here.

Aren't you cold?

It's my blood. Don't bother.

Hard to see how they're feeling with just the eyes.

Meant to be a celebration.

Okay?

INTERPRETER Do you want to continue?

She asks have you children?

ENGLISH No.

INTERPRETER I have a child. Until you have a child you will not know what love you have inside you. Until you know God, you will not know what love you have inside you.

ENGLISH I understand love, and I respect her love.

INTERPRETER You have love inside you now. Inside here. Inside. Inside Hassam's heart. Inside you. Inside God. God inside you. Inside everyone. Inside Hassam. Inside you.

ENGLISH Thank you.

Thank you!

I will do what I can to honour that!

Does she – do you have a photograph. A photograph. Of Hassam?

INTERPRETER Do you have a photograph?

Yes, / I have a photograph.

ENGLISH / Yes! Good. I'd be honoured to see it.

INTERPRETER It is in my bag. With my cousin. / In the lobby.

ENGLISH / Don't worry about it. I just thought it would be / good to see a picture.

INTERPRETER / In my bag.

ENGLISH   No, no. I was just being – It's not important.
            / We could phone down for it. Get your
            cousin –

INTERPRETER / I want to show you. I want you to see
            him. I want you to see his face. I want you
            to understand what has been done.

ENGLISH   Of course.

The wife 'exits'.

Silence.

She got plenty of money, you know.

Silence.

It's been a bit of a year as you can
imagine.

Coming so close to death!

You stop making plans, you know! Getting
strong again, though. Not easy getting used
to the idea, you know. Someone else inside
you! From here! Not easy for people.
Impossible for some to reconcile – You
know. Damaged goods! Imperfect! No
longer me. Not me anymore. Can't accept
it.

A kidney's alright, you know. A liver.

But a heart is more, you know, who you
are, maybe. 'The heart of you.'

Not me anymore, you know. But look.

Look! I feel fine! You wouldn't know,
would you?

Would you? From the outside.

This is meant to be a celebration. My way
of saying thank you.

Closing a chapter.

Wish I had a couple of phrases to say to
her.

It's my life, though.

I mean I got my life back.

Wasn't cheap!

The two actors swap roles.

INTERPRETER	He was twenty-one when the photo was taken.
ENGLISH	Twenty-one. He was very handsome.
INTERPRETER	He was handsome.
ENGLISH	I will frame it.
INTERPRETER	I will frame it.
ENGLISH	Put it in a frame – like this! Put it on my wall! On my wall!
INTERPRETER	I will put it on my wall.
ENGLISH	I will never forget your husband! Hassam.
	He is inside me. I will never forget that!
INTERPRETER	I will never forget Hassam.

Silence.

ENGLISH   Should have brought a photograph of myself!

Please, tell her. If she ever wants to come to London. I will write to her. Send her photographs.

If she needs anything. Anything.

Tell her.

Silence.

We heard that Hassam was in an accident. An accident.

INTERPRETER   Hassam was in an accident.

No. / That's not correct.

ENGLISH   / I'm so sorry. Tell her that I am sure they did everything they could for him.

INTERPRETER   My husband's death was not an accident.

ENGLISH   It is tragic to have a life taken away so suddenly.

INTERPRETER   / No.

ENGLISH   / I have a gift for her. A gift. Tell her. Look. I brought it from England. It will change your life! People think I am crazy but it's important. You gave me my life! Hassam!

Something like this, you know, changes your priorities. Your perspective. A real wake-up call!

INTERPRETER   I have a gift for you.

ENGLISH   Say.

Silence.

INTERPRETER My husband was wounded in the head
and they took him to the nearest hospital
– a private hospital, the Seventh Day
Adventist. It's an expensive hospital. Just
near here.

ENGLISH Okay.

INTERPRETER They told me he was very ill, that he might
die. His family prayed for him – his cousin
came from Berlin, another came from
Paris and from Afghanistan. He was too
ill to move. I went to see him. My father
came with me. My husband's eyes were
open a little.

His brain had been damaged. They would
have to wait if it would get better. The
brain can make itself better.

ENGLISH Right.

INTERPRETER The hospital was very expensive. His
cousin tried to raise money to keep
him there. We had nothing. It was very
difficult. And then a phone call from a
surgeon at another clinic. A private clinic.
In another city. He had been told about
my husband. I thought he was offering to
help him. To save his life.

I was told that someone had offered to
fly my husband to this other clinic. In a
helicopter. The doctors told me there was
a good chance Hassam would recover so
I was happy to let him go. But then I was
visited by an agent from the clinic in the
other city. He told me that my husband
was brain-dead, and that there was a client

55

of the clinic who was prepared to pay me money if I would permit his organs to be used.

Silence.

ENGLISH   I came to give her a gift, a present, tell her.

INTERPRETER   You don't have to do any of this. You don't have to continue with this. We can stop this if you want.

I wanted to see you. I wanted to ask you.

Why has this has happened? Why was my husband killed? / I want to know what he had done wrong. Please tell me.

ENGLISH   / Your husband wasn't killed. He was dying. He would have died. Like me! There was nothing anyone could do for him. It was for the best.

INTERPRETER   Your husband was not killed.

Yes yes.

I was told that he would live.

ENGLISH   It's difficult. The doctors can't always know. Even in my country!

INTERPRETER   A mistake.

No no no.

She's very upset. She says her husband was murdered. Everyone says he was murdered. There is great anger in his family.

ENGLISH   She doesn't understand. Tell her. Tell her. She
          doesn't know what I'm saying. Say what
          I'm saying.

          What have you been saying to her? How
          can she understand if you won't say what
          I'm saying.

INTERPRETER   I have been.

          You can stop this if you want.

          The agent offered me 300,000 if I would
          give permission for my husband's heart
          to be taken. I couldn't believe that my
          husband was dead. I was told he would
          recover. His eyes were open. I forbade
          the operation. The agent told me that my
          husband could save a life. He said that
          to save the life of one man is to save the
          whole of mankind. He offered me half
          a million for my husband's heart. I was
          confused. I had nothing. My father was ill.
          My husband wasn't dead. I signed a paper.
          There was an American.

ENGLISH   Her husband was not killed. He wasn't
          murdered.

          I came to thank her.

          Tell her.

INTERPRETER   She understands that.

I want to know where my husband is. I want to wash him, to prepare him. It is a year now.

The following speeches are played over each other.

INTERPRETER   In my country the dead body must be looked after. He is not a martyr. He is not. I have to have his body. I cannot live not knowing where my husband is. There is no place for my grief. It is unbearable. Intolerable. No wife should have to live with what I have had to live with. I am young. I have nothing. I received no money – a little for phone calls. The money went to the agent, I think. I am a woman alone. I have nothing. My father is ill. I have nothing.

ENGLISH   They said her husband was dead – not dead – that he was being kept alive – just for me. They said nothing else. They said nothing about moving him from anywhere. They said all the paperwork was correct. We paid a lot of money. For the transport and the operation. My friend dealt with it, really. I just saw the airport and the inside of the hospital, that's all. And when I was strong enough, they flew me back to London for recuperation. Privately. I didn't know. I didn't know. I am still weak. I came here for her, tell her, for her.

Overlap ends.

She got money, tell her. She signed.

Fucking tell her that.

What did she say?

INTERPRETER   She says that death is God-given.

ENGLISH   I came to make a reconciliation. I came to meet – to understand what's inside me. To learn. I didn't ask to have your husband inside me. I had no say in it. I was dying and now I'm alive.

Surely that's a good thing. Life is better than death. Look. Instead of both of us being dead, one of us is alive.

I'm alive! Look!

If it had been the other way round it would have been fine. If there was no alternative.

INTERPRETER   Look. I'm alive. I was going to die but now I'm alive.

ENGLISH   Tell her to stop it.

Nobody killed your husband.

I'm really sorry for you. At least he didn't die for nothing, you know. He could be just one of countless others, you know? In the floods or whatever, you know? At least this way his death had a – something came from it.

Tell her.

Tell her.

INTERPRETER   We should stop this.

ENGLISH   I didn't start this. I didn't come here to be accused.

How am I meant to have a proper conversation when I can't even –

Silence.

INTERPRETER   I never saw my husband again. When they moved him. Never again.

Silence.

She's saying that it wasn't an accident. Last year, there were – Her husband was injured in an explosion.

An explosion outside the Marriott. It killed an American official.

ENGLISH   I didn't know. Nobody told me.

I'm sorry.

How many dollars is half a million?

INTERPRETER   Eight thousand.

ENGLISH   And what's the average wage here?

I have a present, a gift, to thank you, to say thank you. To help you.

I brought it from England.

INTERPRETER   I have a gift for you.

ENGLISH   It's a work of art.

INTERPRETER   A work of art.

ENGLISH   It's worth a lot of money.

It's beautiful.

You can do what you like with it. Sell it or keep it. It's yours. A lot of money. For food, or clothes, or water. For your village. For whatever you want.

A lot of money.

Does she understand? I want her to have it. I didn't have to come here. Nobody made me. This is my gift. My thank you.

For my life.

INTERPRETER   A work of art from England.

ENGLISH   It's yours.

Look.

INTERPRETER   She asks if she can listen to you. If she can listen at your chest.

ENGLISH   Of course.

Here.

Silence.

INTERPRETER   She says that she recognises her husband. She can hear her husband.

He is inside you.

ENGLISH   That's good, is it?

INTERPRETER	She says she wishes you were dead so that her husband were alive.
ENGLISH	I'm sorry.
INTERPRETER	I'm sorry.

Silence.

She asks if she can hold you.

| ENGLISH | What? |
| INTERPRETER | Touch you. She asks if she can touch you. |

Silence.

| ENGLISH | What's she saying? |

What?

What's she saying?

What did she say?

What did she say?

Sound – from the other space – which leads the audience away.

End.